The Story of Honey

It Starts with a Flower

Robin Nelson

Lerner Publications ◆ Minneapolis

Lerner Publications Company
An imprint of Lerner Publishing Group, Inc.
241 First Avenue North
Minneapolis, MN 55401 USA

For reading levels and more information, look up this title at www.lernerbooks.com.

Image credits: ktaylorg/iStock/Getty Images, p. 3; Flower_Garden/Shutterstock.com, p. 5; LasART/iStock/Getty Images, pp. 7, 23 (bee); ajma_pl/iStock/Getty Images, pp. 9, 23 (nectar); Thomas Uhlemann/EyeEm/Getty Images, p. 11; weter78/Shutterstock.com, p. 13; Kosolovskyy/iStock/Getty Images, pp. 15, 23 (beekeeper) (honeycomb); Peter Muller/Cultura/Getty Images, p. 17; Hachi888/Shutterstock.com, p. 19; RobertoDavid/iStock/Getty Images, p. 21; IPGGutenbergUKLtd/iStock/Getty Images, p. 22. Cover: Dennis Lane/Getty Images (honey); LightShaper/iStock/Getty Images (bee).

Main body text set in Mikado a Medium.
Typeface provided by HVD Fonts.

Editor: Alison Lorenz **Designer:** Lauren Cooper
Lerner team: Andrea Nelson, Katy Prozinski

Library of Congress Cataloging-in-Publication Data

Names: Nelson, Robin, 1971- author.
Title: The story of honey : it starts with a flower / Robin Nelson.
Description: Minneapolis : Lerner Publications, 2021 | Series: Step by step | Includes
    bibliographical references and index. | Audience: Ages 4-8 | Audience: Grades K-1 |
    Summary: "Honey is a sweet treat! But where does it come from? Colorful photos and
    simple text walk readers through the process"– Provided by publisher.
Identifiers: LCCN 2019045753 (print) | LCCN 2019045754 (ebook) | ISBN 9781541597730
    (library binding) | ISBN 9781728401126 (ebook)
Subjects: LCSH: Honey—Juvenile literature. | Honeybee—Juvenile literature. | Bee culture—
    Juvenile literature.
Classification: LCC SF539 .N45 2021 (print) | LCC SF539 (ebook) | DDC 638/.1—dc23

LC record available at https://lccn.loc.gov/2019045753
LC ebook record available at https://lccn.loc.gov/2019045754

Manufactured in the United States of America
1-47918-48364-11/25/2019

Honey is a sweet treat.

How is it made?

Flowers open.

A bee flies to
the flowers.

The bee
drinks nectar.

Bees fly home.

Bees store
the nectar.

A beekeeper takes the honeycomb.

The beekeeper
removes the honey.

The beekeeper puts the honey in jars.

The honey is
sent to stores.

Time to eat!

Picture Glossary

bee

beekeeper

honeycomb

nectar

Read More

Hansen, Grace. *How is Honey Made?* Minneapolis: Abdo, 2019.

Ridley, Sarah. *Bee to Honey.* New York: Crabtree, 2018.

Taus-Bolstad, Stacy. *The Story of an Apple: It Starts with a Seed.* Minneapolis: Lerner Publications, 2021.

Index

bee, 6, 8, 10, 12

beekeeper, 14, 16, 18

flower, 4, 6

honey, 3, 16, 18, 20

honeycomb, 14

nectar, 8, 12